Preslie the Prissy Pig
Written and Illustrated
by Lori Kaiser

Another great book in the Xavier Series!

Published by
Carpe Diem Publishers
17401 Betty Blvd.
Canyon, TX 79015
806-433-6321

www.carpediempublishers.com

© Copyright, 2011 by Carpe Diem Publishers. All Rights Reserved. No portion of this book may be reproduced, stored in a retrieval system, or transmitted, in any form or by any means, electronic, mechanical, photocopying, recording, or otherwise without prior written permission from publisher.
Printed in the United States of America
ISBN 978-0-9836651-0-6

To the most beautiful niece
in the whole world.
I love you.

She was proper as could be,
and always said, "It's all about me."

She heard a voice in the next stall say, "Hey there, Preslie, you're wasting your days."

Preslie then realized that Sally was right. She didn't want that fate and would now change her life.

www.ingramcontent.com/pod-product-compliance
Lightning Source LLC
Chambersburg PA
CBHW042045290426
44109CB00001B/41